DAY FOR NIGHT

by Kirsten Anderson

PEARSON

Scott
Foresman

Editorial Offices: Glenview, Illinois • Parsippany, New Jersey • New York, New York
Sales Offices: Needham, Massachusetts • Duluth, Georgia • Glenview, Illinois
Coppell, Texas • Ontario, California • Mesa, Arizona

ISBN: 0-328-13448-1

11 V0FL 15 14 13 12 11

CONTENTS

CHAPTER 1 SUN, MOON, AND STARS

Suppose you are on a camping trip. You have been hiking all day and now it is night. After a long day's journey, you set up camp and sit in front of a campfire. The heat warms your face. The **brilliant** colors of the flames light up the area in front of you.

Now turn around. Your back is to the fire. Your face is cold. The world in front of you is dark. You were able to turn your world from day to night. You look up at the stars. How does the sky turn from day to night?

Thousands of years ago, people also looked up at the sky. They watched the movement of the sun. They saw the moon. Small planets **gleamed** in the distance. **Shimmering** stars faded in the dawn. People wondered how the universe worked.

At night the moon seems to shine.

CHAPTER 2 CENTER OF THE UNIVERSE

It was A.D. 150. Ptolemy was a Greek astronomer, or someone who studied objects and matter in outer space. He thought Earth was at the center of a giant circle. The sun, moon, stars, and other planets were all set in the circle. They traveled around the circle. Most people agreed with Ptolemy's ideas about Earth being the center of the universe.

Ptolemy thought that objects in space moved at the same speed and at the same time around Earth.

Nicolaus Copernicus was a Polish astronomer in the early 1500s. He was asked to help make a new calendar. It needed to match days with the movements of the sun and moon.

Copernicus began to think Ptolemy was wrong. The movement of the planets didn't seem right. Copernicus imagined another universe.

Copernicus did not agree with Ptolemy.

Copernicus pictured the sun at the center of the universe. The planets moved around the sun. They traveled at different speeds. This made more sense to Copernicus.

It took a long time for people to accept Copernicus's ideas. In the 1600s the German astronomer Johannes Kepler wrote about the planets and their movements. He agreed with Copernicus. Galileo, a scientist from Italy, used a telescope to prove Copernicus was right.

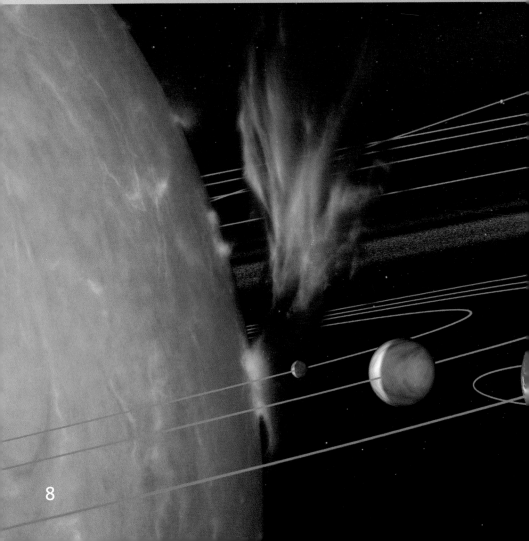

The sun is the center of the solar system.

Powerful people became angry. They wanted Galileo to say Copernicus was wrong. Galileo believed he was right and did not want to be a **coward.** He refused and was banned from publishing his writings.

Copernicus, Kepler, and Galileo were right. By the end of the 1600s, most people believed that Earth moved around the sun.

Earth's place in the universe helps explain a lot about day and night. It helps us understand why some days are longer than others.

EARTH

CHAPTER 3 LIGHT AND DARK

Earth follows a path around the sun. The path is called an orbit. The orbit is oval-shaped. Earth takes about 365 days, or one year, to move around the sun.

Earth spins on its axis at the same time that it travels around the sun. The axis is an imaginary line that runs through Earth.

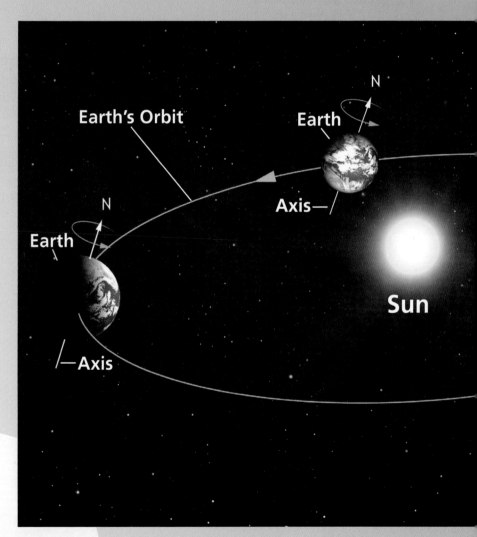

Earth's Orbit

N

Earth

Axis—

N

Earth

—Axis

Sun

Earth spins on its axis like a top. It takes twenty-four hours to make one complete turn. During this turn, each part of Earth faces the sun, making the day. After turning away from the sun, it is night. Day and night make one cycle.

The axis tilts on an angle. It keeps Earth on a tilt. This means that, during the orbit, the North Pole and the South Pole are each tilted toward the sun for half of the orbit.

Earth is always tilted at the same angle on its axis as it travels around the sun.

At the top of Earth are the North Pole and the Arctic Circle. At the bottom of Earth are the South Pole and Antarctica. The tilt means that for six months, or during half of Earth's orbit around the sun, one pole always has some light. At that pole, daylight lasts longer and longer as Earth travels around the sun. This is because the pole is tilted toward the sun.

Finally, there is a point where the sun's rays directly hit the pole. Then that pole has days of complete sunlight. At the same time, the other pole has days of complete darkness. Earth keeps moving in its orbit. Six months pass. Then the other pole faces the sun. It too will have full days of sunlight.

The sun never sets on this day in the Arctic Circle.

CHAPTER 4 THEY LIVE BY NIGHT

Now suppose you're back at your campfire. At night, the trees, rocks, and grass are the same as they were during the day. But at night there are new sounds. You hear a **chorus** of crickets chirp. Bats fly in the dark sky. The animal world has changed.

Bats take to the night sky.

Mammals, reptiles, and insects have patterns to their lives. Some live their lives during the day. They wake up as the sun rises. They feel hungry when it is light. They are active. When it gets dark, they become sleepy. These are *diurnal* creatures. Horses, dogs, lizards, and butterflies are some diurnal creatures.

Nocturnal means "to live by night." Nocturnal creatures sleep during the day. At night they come out and look for food. Bats, owls, moths, hamsters, raccoons, and tree frogs are all nocturnal creatures.

The raccoon is a nocturnal creature.

Why are some species nocturnal? Long ago small animals and reptiles hid during the day to avoid predators. At night there was less competition for them to find food.

Others responded to the climate. Desert creatures hid during the hot day. They came out for food during cool nights. As a result, nocturnal creatures became adapted for night. Some have eyes that are made for darkness. Others, such as bats and rodents, use their senses of hearing and smell to help them in the dark.

You are back at your campfire. It's dark. Your place on Earth has turned away from the sun. But Earth keeps spinning on its axis. It will take you back to the day. This is the cycle of Earth.

Glossary

brilliant *adj.* shining brightly; sparkling.

chorus *n.* anything spoken or sung at the same time.

coward *n.* a person or animal that lacks courage or is easily made afraid.

gleamed *v.* flashed or beamed with light.

shimmering *adj.* gleaming faintly.